WORLD'S STRANGEST

OCEAN BEASTS

Produced for Lonely Planet by Plum5 Limited
Authors: Stuart Derrick & Charlotte Goddard
Editor: Plum5 Limited
Designer: Plum5 Limited
Publishing Director: Piers Pickard
Art Director: Andy Mansfield
Commissioning Editors: Catharine Robertson, Jen Feroze
Assistant Editor: Christina Webb
Print Production: Nigel Longuet, Lisa Ford

Published in August 2018 by Lonely Planet Global Ltd

CRN: 554153
ISBN: 978 1 78701 301 8

www.lonelyplanetkids.com
© Lonely Planet 2018

Printed in China
2 4 6 8 10 9 7 5 3 1

STAY IN TOUCH – lonelyplanet.com/contact
Lonely Planet Offices

AUSTRALIA The Malt Store, Level 3, 551 Swanston St, Carlton, Victoria 3053   T: 03 8379 8000

IRELAND Digital Depot, Roe Lane (off Thomas St), Digital Hub, Dublin 8, D08 TCV4

USA 124 Linden St, Oakland, CA 94607 T: 510 250 6400

UK 240 Blackfriars Rd, London SE1 8NW T: 020 3771 5100

WORLD'S STRANGEST

OCEAN BEASTS

Stuart Derrick &
Charlotte Goddard

PICTURE CREDITS

CONTENTS

INTRODUCTION

More than 70 per cent of our planet is covered in seawater, and our oceans contain millions of amazing creatures. Join us to find out about the most fascinating and creepy creatures, and learn which is the weirdest of them all.

We've ranked the world's strangest ocean beasts to find out about...

⭐ Their crazy skills

⭐ Their bizarre habits

⭐ Their jaw-dropping looks

In this book, you're about to meet:

⭐ The biggest animal that the world has ever known

⭐ A creature with eyes on the end of its arms

⭐ A colour-changing master of disguise

⭐ A fish wearing lipstick

⭐ The fashion designer of the sea

... and many more!

STRANGEOMETER

The creatures in this book are all unique in their own ways, so we've used a special strangeometer to rank them against each other. This is made up of four categories with a mark out of 25 for each.

These categories are...

STRANGEOMETER

APPEARANCE		17/25
WEIRD ABILITIES		8/25
RARITY		12/25
STRANGENESS		13/25
STRANGEOMETER SCORE		50/100

APPEARANCE

This considers how stunning the ocean creature looks.

WEIRD ABILITIES

This considers how What unusual skills does the creature have that make it stand out from the crowd?

RARITY

How likely are you to encounter this creature? Some are very rare indeed!

STRANGENESS

What is the 'wow factor' for this underwater creature?

STRANGEOMETER SCORE

These are added up to get a strangeometer score out of 100!

#40

Although it usually swims slowly, the shark can jump completely out of the water, probably to try to get rid of parasites on its skin.

BASKING SHARK

The big-mouthed basking shark is the second-biggest fish in the seas, however it survives by eating some of the ocean's smallest creatures: plankton.

I CAN FILTER 2,000 TONNES OF SEAWATER AN HOUR. GULP!

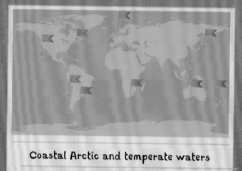

Coastal Arctic and temperate waters

STRANGEOMETER

🐟	APPEARANCE	12/25
⚡	WEIRD ABILITIES	11/25
❓	RARITY	12/25
👁	STRANGENESS	11/25
⭐	STRANGEOMETER SCORE	46/100

#39 TRUMPETFISH

These fish often swim vertically with their heads pointing downwards, trying to blend in with coral. They also disguise themselves as floating sticks to surprise the small reef fish that they eat.

STRANGEOMETER

APPEARANCE		14/25
WEIRD ABILITIES		14/25
RARITY		4/25
STRANGENESS		15/25
STRANGEOMETER SCORE		47/100

The clever trumpetfish can change colour to look like its prey. This allows it to get really close before grabbing its dinner.

CAN I STICK WITH YOU?

Trumpetfish often hitch a ride with larger fish, swimming beside them to sneak up on prey or protect themselves from predators.

Tropical waters of western Atlantic Ocean and Caribbean Sea

Some sea pens can grow up to 2m (6.5ft) tall, but most are smaller than this.

Most sea pens glow when they are touched.

Worldwide

CAN I BE YOUR PEN PAL?

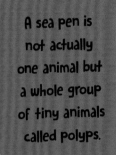

A sea pen is not actually one animal but a whole group of tiny animals called polyps.

STRANGEOMETER

APPEARANCE		18/25
WEIRD ABILITIES		13/25
? RARITY		2/25
STRANGENESS		15/25
⭐ STRANGEOMETER SCORE		48/100

SEA PEN

Sea pens look like old-fashioned quill pens sticking out of the sea bed.

SEA CUCUMBER

When they think they are going to be attacked, some sea cucumbers spurt out sticky threads to trap their enemies.

#37

There are around 1,250 types of sea cucumber. Despite the name, many of them don't really look like the cucumbers we eat. They can be covered in spikes, spots or warts. They move about in herds.

DID SOMEONE MENTION SEAFOOD SALAD?

Sea cucumbers can throw their own guts out of their body to distract predators, giving them time to escape. Their missing body parts grow back later!

STRANGEOMETER

APPEARANCE		13/25
WEIRD ABILITIES		18/25
RARITY		3/25
STRANGENESS		15/25
STRANGEOMETER SCORE		49/100

13

Like many corals, wire coral comes in lots of different colours – from yellow and red to blue and green.

I'M A BIT TIED UP AT THE MOMENT.

Tropical and subtropical seas

WIRE CORAL

As the name of this beautiful form of coral suggests, wire coral can be found in long strands or coils floating in tropical and subtropical seas.

STRANGEOMETER

APPEARANCE		17/25
WEIRD ABILITIES		8/25
RARITY		12/25
STRANGENESS		13/25
STRANGEOMETER SCORE		50/100

They can grow to more than 3m (9ft) in length.

Many tiny creatures such as shrimp make their homes on wire coral.

#35

South Pacific and Indian Oceans

GIANT CLAM

Giant clams really are pretty big – they can be more than 1m (3.3ft) in size and weigh more than 200kg (440lb). They are the largest molluscs on Earth.

STRANGEOMETER

APPEARANCE		13/25
WEIRD ABILITIES		8/25
RARITY		16/25
STRANGENESS		14/25
STRANGEOMETER SCORE		51/100

I CAN LIVE FOR MORE THAN 100 YEARS.

Clams can make pearls, and they are huge too. The biggest one ever found weighed 34kg (75lb). It was found by a fisherman in the Philippines who kept it under his bed as he didn't know that it was worth up to £76 million!

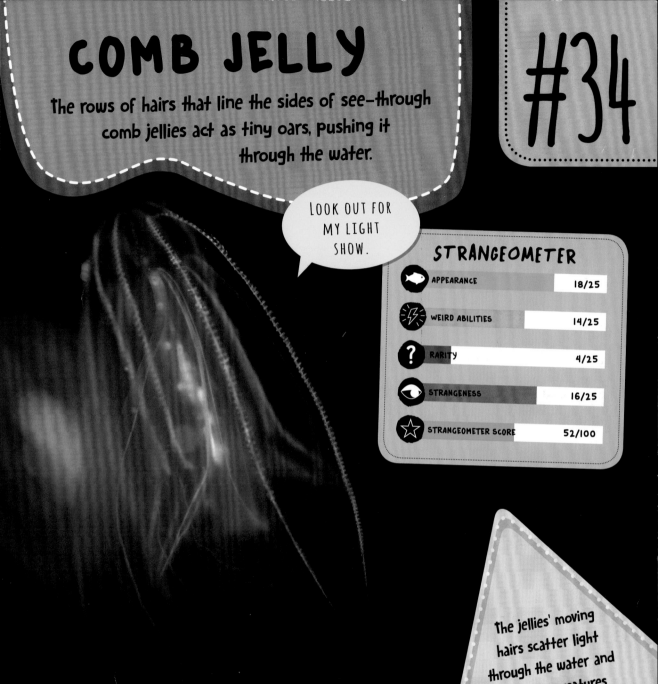

COMB JELLY

The rows of hairs that line the sides of see-through comb jellies act as tiny oars, pushing it through the water.

LOOK OUT FOR MY LIGHT SHOW.

STRANGEOMETER

APPEARANCE		18/25
WEIRD ABILITIES		14/25
RARITY		4/25
STRANGENESS		16/25
STRANGEOMETER SCORE		52/100

The jellies' moving hairs scatter light through the water and make the creatures look like they are covered in rainbows.

Comb jellies are ancient creatures, and have roamed the sea for at least 500 million years. They use a sort of glue to stick their prey to their tentacles, before bringing the unlucky victim to their mouth and eating it.

Worldwide

#33

When a sunfish has too many parasites living on its skin it pays a visit to a seagull. The gull pecks them off, leaving the sunfish nice and clean.

Ocean sunfish can grow as big as a car. They spend half the day sunbathing, which is how they got their name.

Temperate and tropical waters

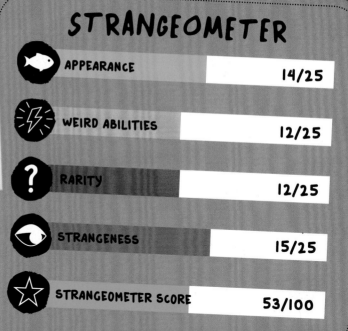

STRANGEOMETER

APPEARANCE		14/25
WEIRD ABILITIES		12/25
RARITY		12/25
STRANGENESS		15/25
STRANGEOMETER SCORE		53/100

MAKE SURE YOU PHOTOGRAPH MY BEST SIDE.

OCEAN SUNFISH

Sunfish produce more eggs than any other backboned animal – up to 300 million at a time.

STRANGEOMETER

APPEARANCE	17/25
WEIRD ABILITIES	16/25
? RARITY	3/25
STRANGENESS	18/25
★ STRANGEOMETER SCORE	54/100

Seahorses have no teeth or stomachs. They suck up food through their snouts like a vacuum cleaner. Baby seahorses eat an amazing 3,000 pieces of food a day!

Male and female seahorses pair for life. Every morning the couple meet up and dance together for up to an hour.

SHALL WE DANCE?

SEAHORSE

Seahorse males give birth to the babies. The female lays eggs in a pocket-like pouch on the male's body, and two to six weeks later baby seahorses are born.

Tropical waters around the world

I'M VERY TASTY – BUT DON'T TELL ANYBODY!

Caribbean Sea, North Atlantic and Indo-Pacific Oceans

STRANGEOMETER

APPEARANCE		15/25
WEIRD ABILITIES		15/25
RARITY		12/25
STRANGENESS		13/25
STRANGEOMETER SCORE		55/100

RED LIONFISH

A lionfish can deliver venom through up to 18 needle-like fins. Its sting is extremely painful to humans but doesn't usually kill them.

Lionfish are invading seas around the United States and Europe, taking over from the fish that already live there. In the US people are being encouraged to eat lionfish, to get rid of them!

Lionfish sometimes spread their fins and herd small fish into tight corners, so they can eat them more easily.

QUIZ

See if you can answer these questions on the ten ocean beasts you've just learned about!

3. What do most sea pens do when touched?

How many types of sea cucumber are there?

1. What is this fish?

4.

How does the trumpetfish sneak up on its prey?

2.

What is this mollusc?

6. How long have comb jellies been on Earth?

8. How many eggs does a sunfish produce?

7.

5. How long can wire coral grow?

10. What can a lionfish do with its needle-like fins?

9.

What do male and female seahorses do every morning?

Caribbean and Gulf of Mexico,
Amazon basin, West Africa

These gentle mammals are also called sea cows, and are found in coastal waters and rivers. They feed on grass, algae and weeds.

Manatees 'walk' on the bottom of the sea with their flippers.

MANATEE

When explorer Christopher Columbus first saw manatees, he thought they were mermaids. He was a bit disappointed that they weren't as beautiful as he thought mermaids would be.

SEA COW? I'M ACTUALLY RELATED TO ELEPHANTS I'LL HAVE YOU KNOW!

Manatees never leave the water, but they have to breathe air above the surface.

STRANGEOMETER

APPEARANCE		17/25
WEIRD ABILITIES		10/25
RARITY		14/25
STRANGENESS		15/25
STRANGEOMETER SCORE		56/100

Come and see me on the ocean bed.

South Pacific Ocean, South Atlantic Ocean and Indian Ocean

STRANGEOMETER

APPEARANCE		22/25
WEIRD ABILITIES		15/25
RARITY		3/25
STRANGENESS		17/25
STRANGEOMETER SCORE		57/100

SEA PIG

These chubby little fellows are very common indeed – but most people will never see one, as they live right at the very bottom of the ocean.

The creatures are a type of sea cucumber and are related to starfish and sea urchins.

Sea pigs have five to seven pairs of feet and get around by walking on the sea floor. They also have feet on their heads.

Sea pigs like to hang out in big groups, and when they are in a crowd, they all face in the same direction.

STRANGEOMETER

APPEARANCE		21/25
WEIRD ABILITIES		8/25
RARITY		13/25
STRANGENESS		16/25
STRANGEOMETER SCORE		58/100

DO YOU FANCY A SLEEPOVER?

Western, southern and eastern Australian coasts

STRIPED PYJAMA SQUID

This creature looks like it's dressed ready for bed. Despite its name, it's not really a squid – it's a cuttlefish. Being small and round, it is also often referred to as a striped dumpling squid.

The striped pyjama squid likes to bury itself in sand so only the top of its head is visible. This helps it catch its prey by surprise – boo!

The striped pyjama squid is about 5cm (2in) long and lives in waters that are up to 20m (65ft) deep.

Hawaii, Africa, the Red Sea, southern Japan, the Philippines and Australia

STRANGEOMETER

APPEARANCE		19/25
WEIRD ABILITIES		15/25
RARITY		8/25
STRANGENESS		17/25
STRANGEOMETER SCORE		59/100

MY FRIENDS JUST CALL ME HUMUHUMU!

Reef triggerfish use their spines to lock themselves into small cracks in rocks, making it hard for predators to pull them out. When the predator is gone, the triggerfish pulls in its spines and swims off.

REEF TRIGGERFISH

The reef triggerfish is also known by its Hawaiian name, Humuhumunukunukuāpua'a, pronounced who-moo-who-moo-noo-koo-noo-koo-ah-pooah-ah. This means 'triggerfish with a snout like a pig'.

LONGHORN COWFISH #26

Southern Africa and Indo-Pacific region

The long horns on a cowfish's head mean predators find it difficult to swallow. The horns break off easily but can grow back after a few months. The cowfish also releases a poisonous chemical when it gets scared.

I HOVER LIKE A SPACESHIP WHEN I SWIM.

STRANGEOMETER

APPEARANCE		19/25
WEIRD ABILITIES		17/25
RARITY		5/25
STRANGENESS		19/25
STRANGEOMETER SCORE		60/100

Cowfish swim so slowly it's easy to catch them by hand. They blow jets of water at the sand on coral reefs to reveal their prey, and make loud grunts when they're scared.

BLUE WHALE

The blue whale is the biggest creature in the world. In fact, experts think that it is the biggest animal that has ever existed.

I CAN SWIM AT 32KPH (20MPH).

The blue whale is also the loudest creature in the world. Its cry can be louder than a jet engine, and scientists think blue whales can hear each other up to 1,600km (1,000mi) apart.

Antarctic, North Pacific, Indian Ocean, North Atlantic

Despite their size, blue whales eat mainly tiny creatures, known as krill. But they eat a lot of them – up to 40 million a day.

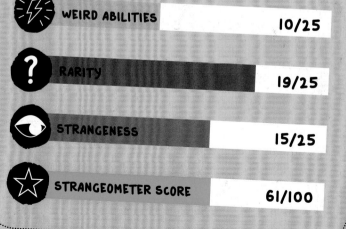

STRANGEOMETER

APPEARANCE		17/25
WEIRD ABILITIES		10/25
RARITY		19/25
STRANGENESS		15/25
STRANGEOMETER SCORE		61/100

SEA ANGEL

These fairy-like creatures hover in the water, never touching the bottom or coming to the surface.

One type of sea angel oozes a special chemical which predators don't like. A shrimp-like creature called *Hyperiella dilatata* takes advantage of this by kidnapping sea angels and putting them on its back – then it is protected, too!

I'M REALLY A KIND OF SEA SLUG.

Sea angels are tiny and almost completely see-through. They only grow to about 5cm (2in) in length.

STRANGEOMETER

APPEARANCE		18
WEIRD ABILITIES		18
RARITY		8
STRANGENESS		18
STRANGEOMETER SCORE		62

Arctic Ocean, and cold waters of the North Pacific and North Atlantic Oceans

Like other octopuses, dumbos can swim by jet propulsion. They shoot out jets of water to push themselves along.

Worldwide

I LIVE DEEPER IN THE OCEAN THAN ANY OTHER OCTOPUS.

The largest dumbo octopus ever recorded was 1.8m (6ft) long and weighed 5.9kg (13lb).

STRANGEOMETER

APPEARANCE		20/25
WEIRD ABILITIES		13/25
RARITY		10/25
STRANGENESS		20/25
STRANGEOMETER SCORE		63/100

DUMBO OCTOPUS

These octopuses were named after the cartoon elephant Dumbo because of the fins that stick out of their heads like big ears. They flap their 'ears' to glide through the dark depths where they live – 3,000m (9,800ft) below the surface.

Sloane's viperfish can produce light with their bodies to attract prey.

STRANGEOMETER

APPEARANCE 22/25

WEIRD ABILITIES 18/25

? RARITY 6/25

STRANGENESS 18/25

☆ STRANGEOMETER SCORE 64/100

The Sloane's viperfish lives at depths of up to 2,500m (8,200ft), so scientists haven't been able to study it very much.

Tropical and temperate waters

AT NIGHT I SWIM UP
TO SHALLOWER WATERS
TO FIND MY FOOD.

Although they
look scary,
they are not
dangerous
to humans.

SLOANE'S VIPERFISH

Sloane's viperfish have bigger teeth compared to the size of their head than any other fish. Their huge fangs don't fit inside their closed mouths, so they curve upward towards their eyes.

Sunflower sea stars have 16 to 24 arms and can be bright orange, yellow, red, brown or sometimes purple. They have no eyes, brain or blood, but they have eye-like organs on the tips of their arms.

STRANGEOMETER

APPEARANCE		20/25
WEIRD ABILITIES		18/25
RARITY		5/25
STRANGENESS		22/25
STRANGEOMETER SCORE		65/100

SUNFLOWER SEA STAR

Northeast Pacific

The sunflower sea star is one of the world's largest and fastest-moving starfish. It can move at 1m (3.3ft) per minute and can grow up to 1m (3.3ft) long.

I CAN SHED AN ARM TO ESCAPE FROM A PREDATOR AND THEN GROW IT BACK.

Like all sea stars, they can push their stomachs out through their mouth to catch their prey, so they can eat things that are larger than their mouth.

QUIZ

What is this creature?

4.

1. Where do sea pigs have extra legs?

2. Which animal has fins that look like big ears?

3. What did Christopher Columbus think manatees were?

6. What happens when a longhorn cowfish gets scared?

What is the biggest animal ever to have lived?

7.

8.

5.

How do reef triggerfish avoid being eaten?

What is this fish?

10.

9.

Which fairy-like creature is actually a sea slug?

How many arms does the sunflower sea star have?

ANSWERS

I. ON THEIR HEADS 2. A DUMBO OCTOPUS 3. MERMAIDS 4. STRIPED PYJAMA SQUID 5. THEY LOCK THEMSELVES IN ROCK CRACKS WITH THEIR SPINES 6. IT RELEASES POISON 7. THE BLUE WHALE 8. SLOANE'S VIPERFISH 9. THE SEA ANGEL 10. 16-24

#20

The flamingo tongue snail wraps its brightly patterned soft tissue around the outside of its plain white shell. It can hide its colourful body back inside its shell if it is attacked.

Like all snails, flamingo tongue snails eat with their feet.

FLAMINGO TONGUE SNAIL

These creatures eat poisonous sea fans, but that doesn't bother them – they take the poison and put it in their shell, becoming poisonous themselves.

I LIVE FOR ABOUT TWO YEARS.

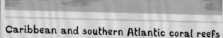

Caribbean and southern Atlantic coral reefs

STRANGEOMETER

APPEARANCE		22/25
WEIRD ABILITIES		20/25
RARITY		6/25
STRANGENESS		18/25
STRANGEOMETER SCORE		66/100

#19

Some scientists think narwhals use their tusks to determine if nearby icebergs are melting by measuring how salty the water is. Others think the tusks are used as weapons.

You can guess a narwhal's age by its colour. Babies are blue-gray and become blue-black, then mottled grey as they get older. By the time they reach old age, narwhals are nearly white.

In the Middle Ages, Vikings used to sell narwhal horns for lots of money to people from more southern countries, pretending they were unicorn horns.

NARWHAL

Narwhals are a type of whale and live in the cold waters of the Arctic. Their amazing tusks never stop growing – they can reach 3m (9ft) long.

FOLLOW THE TUSK!

Arctic waters

STRANGEOMETER

APPEARANCE		24/25
WEIRD ABILITIES		10/25
RARITY		13/25
STRANGENESS		20/25
STRANGEOMETER SCORE		67/100

#18

CHRISTMAS TREE WORM

These beautiful creatures look like multicoloured Christmas trees and live on coral reefs around the world. Once they find a place they like, they burrow into the coral and stay there.

When they are startled, Christmas tree worms quickly pop back inside their burrows.

They have eyes on their gills, which helps them see outside their burrows without having to pop their heads out.

STRANGEOMETER

APPEARANCE		25/25
WEIRD ABILITIES		15/25
? RARITY		5/25
STRANGENESS		23/25
☆ STRANGEOMETER SCORE		68/100

IT'S ALWAYS FESTIVE WHEN WE'RE AROUND!

Pacific and Atlantic Oceans, the Mediterranean Sea and Australia

DECORATOR CRAB

These creative critters are the fashion designers of the sea. They grab items such as seaweed and corals, and stick them onto their shells as camouflage. Everything stays in place thanks to the hooked hairs that line their shells.

DO YOU LIKE MY NEW LOOK?

Tropical coral reefs

Like other crabs, decorator crabs shed their shells to grow. They often recycle their decorations, carefully removing them from their old shell and sticking them on their new one.

Some types of decorator crab choose ornaments that are poisonous or dangerous, like stinging sea anemones, to protect themselves from predators.

STRANGEOMETER

APPEARANCE		22/25
WEIRD ABILITIES		18/25
RARITY		8/25
STRANGENESS		21/25
STRANGEOMETER SCORE		69/100

#16 PARROTFISH

Parrotfish start off as females and then change into males. As they grow up, they also change colour – grown-up parrotfish are brightly coloured, but the young are duller reds, browns and greys.

MY PARROT-LIKE BEAK HELPS ME NIBBLE CORAL.

If you are walking on a beautiful white-sand beach in the Caribbean, you are probably treading on parrotfish poo. Parrotfish eat coral and poo it out as sand!

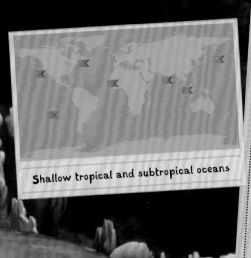

Shallow tropical and subtropical oceans

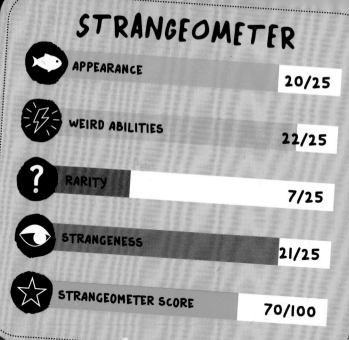

STRANGEOMETER

	APPEARANCE	20/25
	WEIRD ABILITIES	22/25
?	RARITY	7/25
	STRANGENESS	21/25
★	STRANGEOMETER SCORE	70/100

Parrotfish sleep in a cocoon made of their own mucus, which comes from a strange organ on their heads. These bizarre sleeping bags hide them from predators.

#15

Horseshoe crabs have blue blood which scientists use to test new drugs. A litre (1.76 pints) of the blood is worth around $15,000.

STRANGEOMETER

APPEARANCE		23/25
WEIRD ABILITIES		22/25
RARITY		6/25
STRANGENESS		20/25
STRANGEOMETER SCORE		71/100

HORSESHOE CRAB

The horseshoe crab is actually more closely related to spiders than to crabs. While it may not be the most beautiful, it's one of the oldest creatures on Earth.

I'VE LOOKED LIKE THIS FOR 445 MILLION YEARS.

A horseshoe crab has a whopping ten eyes, including one on its tail.

I'M CLOSING A BEACH NEAR YOU SOON.

STRANGEOMETER

APPEARANCE		22/25
WEIRD ABILITIES		20/25
RARITY		10/25
STRANGENESS		20/25
STRANGEOMETER SCORE		72/100

The Portuguese man-of-war gets its name from the balloon-like part that sits above the water and looks a bit like the sail of a ship. It drifts in the ocean, often in groups of hundreds.

Their tentacles are extremely poisonous and can stretch for 50m (164ft).

Atlantic, Pacific and Indian Oceans

PORTUGUESE MAN-OF-WAR

Often mistaken for a jellyfish, the Portuguese man-of-war is actually a colony of different organisms working together.

HAGFISH

#13

These slippery customers cover themselves with slime to protect themselves from being eaten. A single hagfish can fill a bucket with slime in minutes.

I CAN ABSORB FOOD THROUGH MY SKIN

Hagfish have four hearts, at least twice as much blood as other fish, and only half a jaw. They also have very floppy skin.

A hagfish can tie itself into a knot.

Pacific and Atlantic Oceans

STRANGEOMETER

APPEARANCE		22/25
WEIRD ABILITIES		22/25
RARITY		6/25
STRANGENESS		23/25
STRANGEOMETER SCORE		73/100

#12

I SUCK UP FOOD THROUGH MY SNOUT. SLURP!

The tail of a male leafy turns bright yellow when he is ready to mate.

STRANGEOMETER

APPEARANCE	23/25
WEIRD ABILITIES	13/25
RARITY	20/25
STRANGENESS	18/25
STRANGEOMETER SCORE	74/100

LEAFY SEADRAGON

To protect themselves from being eaten, leafy seadragons have evolved to look like seaweed.

Southern Australia

Female leafies put their bright pink eggs on the males' tails, and the male leafies look after them for a month or so until they hatch.

MY SPOTS ARE UNIQUE — JUST LIKE YOUR FINGERPRINTS.

Handfish are a rare kind of anglerfish.

Southern Australia and Tasmania

HANDFISH

Handfish are terrible swimmers. Luckily, they have amazing fins that have developed to look like hands, and they use them to walk across the sea floor.

Fourteen species of handfish have been discovered so far. They grow up to 15cm (6in) long and live in shallow waters off the coasts of Australia and Tasmania.

STRANGEOMETER

APPEARANCE		18/25
WEIRD ABILITIES		17/25
? RARITY		21/25
STRANGENESS		19/25
★ STRANGEOMETER SCORE		75/100

QUIZ

See if you can answer these questions on the ten ocean beasts you've just learned about!

3. How can you tell a narwhal's age?

What do Christmas tree worms do when startled?

1. How do flamingo tongue snails eat?

4.

What is this creature?

2.

6. How do decorator crabs attach things to their shells?

7. What colour is horseshoe crab blood?

8. How long are Portuguese man-of-war tentacles?

5. Where do parrotfish sleep?

What is this fish?

9.

10. What do handfish do with their 'hands'?

ANSWERS

1. WITH THEIR FEET 2. HAGFISH 3. BY ITS COLOUR 4. POP BACK INTO THEIR BURROWS 5. IN A COCOON MADE OF THEIR OWN MUCUS 6. WITH HOOKED HAIRS 7. BLUE 8. UP TO 50M (164FT) 9. LEAFY SEADRAGON 10. WALK WITH THEM

#10

One species of pistol shrimp, *Synalpheus pinkfloydi*, is named after the band Pink Floyd, because of its pink claw and the huge amount of noise it makes.

STRANGEOMETER

APPEARANCE	15/25
WEIRD ABILITIES	25/25
RARITY	11/25
STRANGENESS	25/25
STRANGEOMETER SCORE	76/100

Worldwide

PISTOL SHRIMP

Also known as snapping shrimp, pistol shrimp fire bubble 'bullets' at their enemies. The bubbles reach a speed of 100 mph (160 kph) and make a sound louder than a gunshot.

For a split second, the shrimp's claw heats up the water to a temperature of more than 4,000°C (7,000°F). That's nearly the same temperature as the surface of the Sun!

I'M THE FASTEST GUN IN THE SEA.

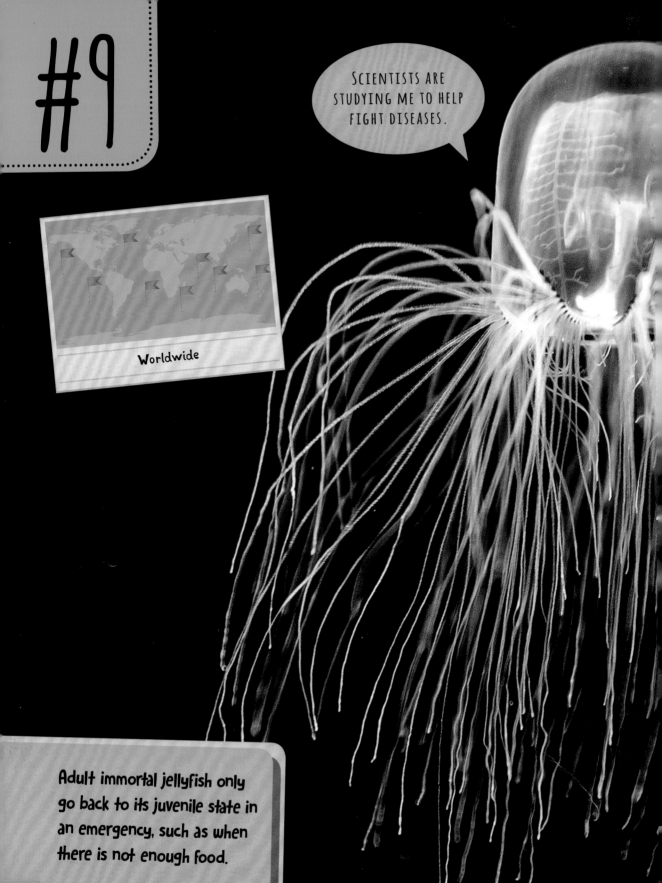

#9

SCIENTISTS ARE STUDYING ME TO HELP FIGHT DISEASES.

Worldwide

Adult immortal jellyfish only go back to its juvenile state in an emergency, such as when there is not enough food.

IMMORTAL JELLYFISH

This tiny jellyfish can live backwards. It can revert from its adult form back to its juvenile polyp form. This means that if it doesn't get eaten, become ill, or have an accident, it could potentially live forever.

Immortal jellyfish are only 4.5mm (0.2in) long.

STRANGEOMETER

APPEARANCE		17/25
WEIRD ABILITIES		25/25
RARITY		10/25
STRANGENESS		25/25
STRANGEOMETER SCORE		77/100

#8 FIREFLY SQUID

Every firefly squid has tiny, light-producing organs all over its body. Between March and June each year, they mass together in seas off the coast of Japan to create amazing blue underwater light shows, like firework displays.

No one is quite sure why the squid light up. It could be to speak to each other, to attract a mate, or to scare predators.

the firefly squid is thought to be the only squid that can see in colour.

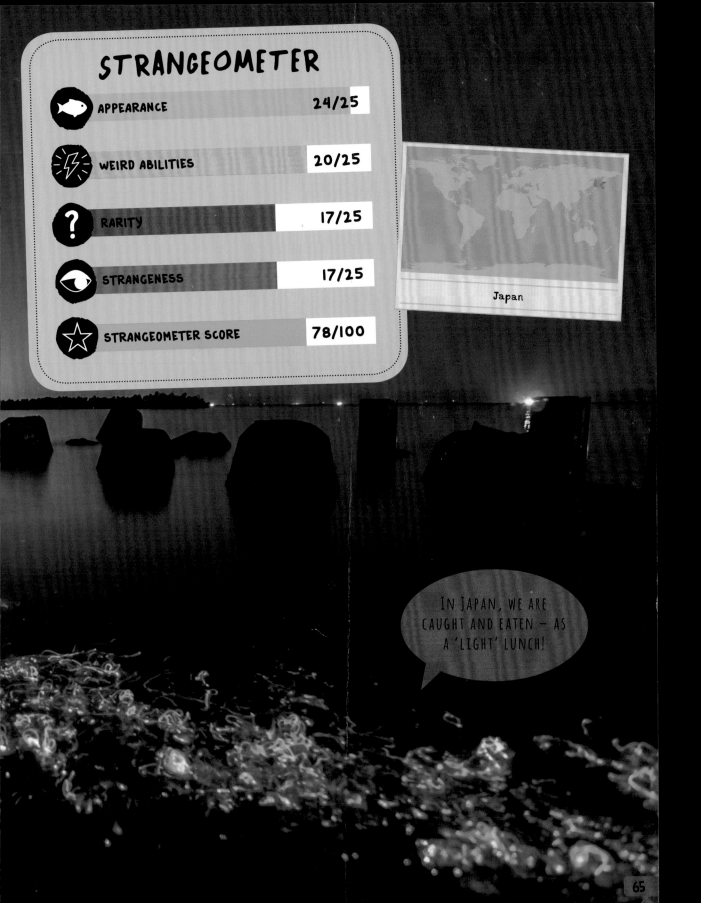

STRANGEOMETER

APPEARANCE		24/25
WEIRD ABILITIES		20/25
RARITY		17/25
STRANGENESS		17/25
⭐ STRANGEOMETER SCORE		78/100

Japan

IN JAPAN, WE ARE CAUGHT AND EATEN — AS A 'LIGHT' LUNCH!

STRANGEOMETER

APPEARANCE		20/25
WEIRD ABILITIES		23/25
? RARITY		15/25
STRANGENESS		21/25
⭐ STRANGEOMETER SCORE		79/100

The shark's body has a natural antifreeze. If you eat its fresh meat, you feel drunk.

MOST OF US ARE ALMOST BLIND BECAUSE OF PARASITES IN OUR EYES.

Sub-Arctic waters

GREENLAND SHARK

This huge shark is the longest-living vertebrate on earth – living for around 400 years. It grows incredibly slowly, at less than 1cm (0.4in) a year.

The Greenland shark is found farther north than any other shark and swims very slowly in the icy waters to save energy.

JAPANESE SPIDER CRAB

The Japanese spider crab measures around 4m (13ft) across. It has eight legs and two long feeding arms, although scientists found that three quarters of the crabs they studied had lost at least one leg.

I'M ACTUALLY QUITE A GENTLE CRAB.

STRANGEOMETER

APPEARANCE		24/25
WEIRD ABILITIES		13/25
RARITY		19/25
STRANGENESS		24/25
STRANGEOMETER SCORE		80/100

This crab may look scary, but you're unlikely to meet one – the gigantic beast lives deep in the Pacific Ocean, between 50–600m (164–12,000ft) down.

Japanese spider crabs are the grandfathers of the sea – they are thought to live for around 100 years.

Pacific Ocean

CLOWN FROGFISH

Sometimes known by the less cute name of the warty frogfish, this creature is a master of disguise. Its skin is covered in lots of little bumps and it can match its colour to the part of the ocean where it lives.

At about 15cm (6in), it's quite small, but the clown frogfish has a big mouth and can swallow prey as big as itself, which can include other frogfish.

STRANGEOMETER

🐟 APPEARANCE		24/25
⚡ WEIRD ABILITIES		23/25
❓ RARITY		11/25
👁 STRANGENESS		23/25
⭐ STRANGEOMETER SCORE		81/100

Divers love photographing them as they stay still for so long that they're easy to snap... if you can spot one.

MY MOVEMENT TO CATCH PREY IS ONE OF THE FASTEST IN THE ANIMAL WORLD.

Tropical and subtropical regions of the Pacific and Atlantic, as well as the Red Sea and Indian Ocean

#4 RED-LIPPED BATFISH

This pouty-lipped fish definitely has a face you'll never forget. But that's not all – its fins have been specially adapted so that it looks as if it walks on the sea bed. It can't actually swim very well.

STRANGEOMETER

APPEARANCE	25/25
WEIRD ABILITIES	20/25
RARITY	17/25
STRANGENESS	20/25
STRANGEOMETER SCORE	82/100

Scientists think that those large, red, kissable lips are designed to attract a mate. They're certainly hard to miss. Mwah!

The batfish also has a long nose which sticks out and is used to attract prey, even if it doesn't attract a mate.

GIVE US A KISS!

Galapagos Islands

GOBLIN SHARK

The alien-looking goblin shark can slide its jaws forward to catch its prey. Its snout can sense movement, which helps it to zero in on nearby fish.

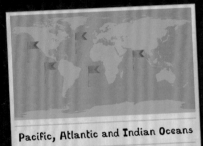

Pacific, Atlantic and Indian Oceans

I'M SOMETIMES CALLED THE VAMPIRE SHARK BECAUSE I AVOID THE LIGHT.

Goblin sharks aren't often seen – they live in very deep waters, more than 0.6 miles (1 km) down. Even if you could swim that far down, the shark probably wouldn't see you because its eyesight is very poor.

The goblin shark has been called a 'living fossil' because it is related to a family of sharks that were around 125 million years ago.

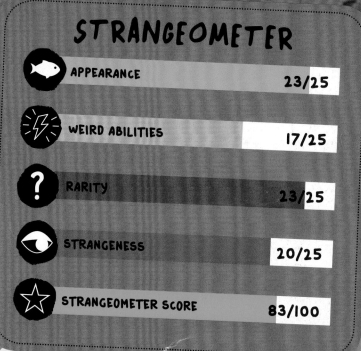

STRANGEOMETER

APPEARANCE		23/25
WEIRD ABILITIES		17/25
RARITY		23/25
STRANGENESS		20/25
STRANGEOMETER SCORE		83/100

#2

To pretend to be a lionfish, the mimic octopus can change colour and shape its eight legs to look like spines.

I WAS ONLY DISCOVERED IN 1998.

MIMIC OCTOPUS

If the ocean had Oscars, the mimic octopus would win them all. If it is being attacked it can change the way it looks and pretend to be other sea creatures, such as lionfish, sea snakes, starfish or jellyfish.

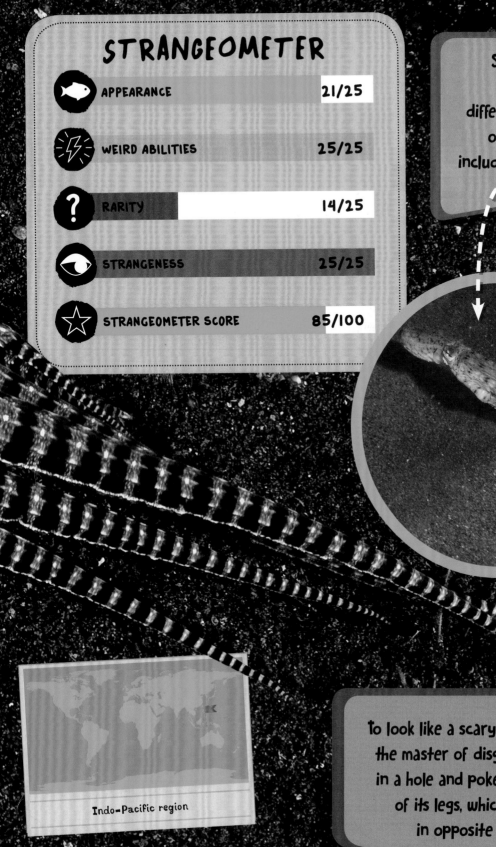

STRANGEOMETER

APPEARANCE		21/25
WEIRD ABILITIES		25/25
RARITY		14/25
STRANGENESS		25/25
STRANGEOMETER SCORE		85/100

Scientists have discovered 15 different disguises of the octopus, including the squid.

Indo-Pacific region

To look like a scary sea snake, the master of disguise hides in a hole and pokes out two of its legs, which it places in opposite directions.

#1

SOME OF US CAN GROW UP TO 1M (3.3FT) IN LENGTH. DON'T HAVE NIGHTMARES!

A piece of the female anglerfish's spine hangs over her head, like a fishing pole with a tasty worm attached. The tip of the pole glows in the dark to attract smaller prey and lure them into the anglerfish's mouth.

STRANGEOMETER

APPEARANCE	23/25	
WEIRD ABILITIES	25/25	
RARITY	13/25	
STRANGENESS	25/25	
STRANGEOMETER SCORE	86/100	

ANGLERFISH

This creepy-looking creature mostly lives at the bottom of the deep, dark Atlantic and Antarctic oceans, and it has some super-weird habits.

Atlantic and Antarctic oceans

Male anglerfish are much smaller than females. When they find a female they latch on to her with their sharp teeth and stick to her, losing their eyes and most of their internal organs. Females can carry six or more males on their bodies.

QUIZ

See if you can answer these questions on the ten ocean beasts you've just learned about!

3.

What is thought to be the only squid that can see in colour?

Why are many Greenland sharks almost blind?

1.

4.

What temperature does the pistol shrimp's claw snap produce?

2.

What is this creature?

6. Why is it easy to take a picture of a clown frogfish?

7.

What is this fish?

5. How big is the Japanese spider crab?

8. What is the goblin shark's nickname?

9.

What does the female angler fish use to attract food?

10. How many disguises does the mimic octopus have?

ANSWERS

1. MORE THAN 4,000 DEGREES CELSIUS (7,000 DEGREES FAHRENHEIT)
2. IMMORTAL JELLYFISH 3. IT HAS PARASITES LIVING IN ITS EYES
4. THE FIREFLY SQUID 5. ABOUT 4M (13FT) ACROSS 6. BECAUSE THEY
STAY VERY STILL 7. RED-LIPPED BATFISH 8. THE VAMPIRE SHARK
9. A FISHING POLE ON HER HEAD 10. AT LEAST 15

GLOSSARY

algae	very small organisms (living things) which look like plants and grow in or near water
colony	a group of animals of the same type living or growing together
coral	a marine animal which stays in one place under the sea and forms a hard rock-like substance
fang	a large pointed tooth
fossil	the remains of an animal or plant, preserved in rock after millions of years
gill	the body part of a fish or marine creature which it uses to breathe
mammal	warm-blooded animals that breathe air; the females have glands that produce milk for their young
Middle Ages	the period of history between about 500 and 1500 AD
mollusc	an animal with no spine and a soft body, often covered in a shell
mucus	the slimy liquid that is produced by the nose
organ	a part of the body
organism	a living thing
parasite	an organism which lives on and feeds off another organism
plankton	really really small plants and animals which float in the sea
polyp	a simple tube-shaped water organism
predator	an animal which hunts and eats other another animals
prey	an animal which is hunted and eaten by another animal
quill pen	a pen made from the feather of a goose or other bird, used in the past
species	a type of animal or plant with similar characteristics
subtropical	the areas which are immediately north or south of the tropics (see tropical)
temperate	a temperature which is neither very hot nor very cold
tentacle	a long thin arm-like part of an animal's body used for catching food, moving around or defence
tropical	relating to the tropics, which is the area on either side of the Equator, the imaginary line around the centre of the Earth
vertebrate	a creature with a spine